I LOVE TO BRUSH MY TEETH
ICH PUTZE MEINE ZÄHNE GERN

Shelley Admont
Illustrated by Sonal Goyal and Sumit Sakhuja

www.kidkiddos.com
Copyright©2014 by S.A.Publishing ©2017 by KidKiddos Books Ltd.
support@kidkiddos.com

All rights reserved. No part of this book may be reproduced in any form or by any electronic or mechanical means, including information storage and retrieval systems, without written permission from the publisher or author, except in the case of a reviewer, who may quote brief passages embodied in critical articles or in a review.

Alle Rechte vorbehalten. Kein Teil dieses Buches darf in irgendeiner Form oder durch irgendwelche elektronischen oder mechanischen Mitteln, einschließlich Informationen Regalbediengeräte schriftlich beim Verlag, mit Ausnahme von einem Rezensenten, kurze Passagen in einer Bewertung zitieren darf reproduziert, ohne Erlaubnis.
Second edition, 2019

Translated from English by Tess Parthum
Aus dem Englischen übersetzt von Tess Parthum

Library and Archives Canada Cataloguing in Publication Data
I love to brush my teeth (German Bilingual Edition)/ Shelley Admont
ISBN: 978-1-5259-1596-3 paperback
ISBN: 978-1-77268-431-5 hardcover
ISBN: 978-1-77268-010-2 ebook

Please note that the German and English versions of the story have been written to be as close as possible. However, in some cases they differ in order to accommodate nuances and fluidity of each language.

For those I love the most—S.A.

Für die, die ich am meisten liebe—S.A.

Morning came and the sun was shining in the faraway forest. There, in a small house, lived little bunny Jimmy, with his parents and two older brothers.

Der Morgen kam und die Sonne schien im weit entfernten Wald. Dort, in einem kleinen Haus, lebte der kleine Hase Jimmy mit seinen Eltern und zwei älteren Brüdern.

Mom came into the room that Jimmy shared with his brothers.

Mama kam ins Zimmer, das Jimmy mit seinen Brüdern teilte.

First she kissed the oldest brother, who slept peacefully in his blue bed.

Zuerst küsste sie den ältesten Bruder, der friedlich in seinem blauen Bett schlief.

Next she gave a kiss to the middle brother. He was still sleeping in his green bed.

Dann gab sie dem mittleren Bruder einen Kuss. Er schlief noch in seinem grünen Bett.

Finally, Mom went to Jimmy's orange bed, and gave him a kiss.

Schließlich ging die Mama zu Jimmys orangefarbenem Bett und gab ihm einen Kuss.

"Good morning, children," said Mom. "It's time to rise."

„Guten Morgen, Kinder", sagte Mama. „Es ist Zeit, aufzustehen."

Getting out of bed, the oldest brother made his way to the bathroom.

Der älteste Bruder stieg aus dem Bett und ging ins Bad.

"Wow!" he shouted, "I have a brand-new toothbrush! It's blue, my favorite color. Thank you, Mom." He started to brush his teeth.

„Wow!", rief er, „Ich habe eine brandneue Zahnbürste! Sie ist blau, meine Lieblingsfarbe. Danke, Mama." Er begann, seine Zähne zu putzen.

The middle brother followed him. "I have a new toothbrush as well, and mine's green!" he exclaimed and also began to brush his teeth.

Der mittlere Bruder folgte ihm. „Ich habe auch eine neue Zahnbürste und meine ist grün!", rief er und fing ebenfalls an, seine Zähne zu putzen.

Jimmy got out of bed and walked slowly towards the bathroom. *Why even bother brushing my teeth?* he thought. *My teeth are fine as they are.*

Jimmy kletterte aus dem Bett und lief langsam zum Badezimmer. Warum soll ich mir überhaupt die Mühe machen, meine Zähne zu putzen? dachte er. Meine Zähne sind gut so, wie sie sind.

"Look, Jimmy," said his oldest brother, "you have a new toothbrush too. It's orange like your bed."

„Schau, Jimmy", sagte sein ältester Bruder, „du hast auch eine neue Zahnbürste. Sie ist orange, wie dein Bett."

"So I have a new toothbrush, big deal." Jimmy stood in front of the mirror, but he still didn't start brushing his teeth.

„Dann habe ich eben eine neue Zahnbürste, na und?" Jimmy stand vor dem Spiegel, aber er fing immer noch nicht an, seine Zähne zu putzen.

"Kids, hurry up! Breakfast is almost ready," they heard their mother's soft voice. "Has everyone finished brushing their teeth?"

„Kinder, beeilt euch, das Frühstück ist fast fertig", hörten sie die leise Stimme ihrer Mutter. „Sind alle fertig mit dem Zähneputzen?"

"I've finished," answered the oldest brother and ran out of the bathroom.

„Ich bin fertig", antwortete der älteste Bruder und rannte aus dem Bad.

"Me too," replied the middle brother. He ran after his brother to the kitchen.

„Ich auch", erwiderte der mittlere Bruder. Er rannte seinem Bruder hinterher in die Küche.

"Mom, I finished brushing my teeth too," shouted Jimmy. He was just about to leave the bathroom, when he heard a voice.

„Mama, ich bin auch fertig mit dem Zähneputzen", rief Jimmy. Er war gerade dabei, aus dem Badezimmer zu gehen, als er eine Stimme hörte.

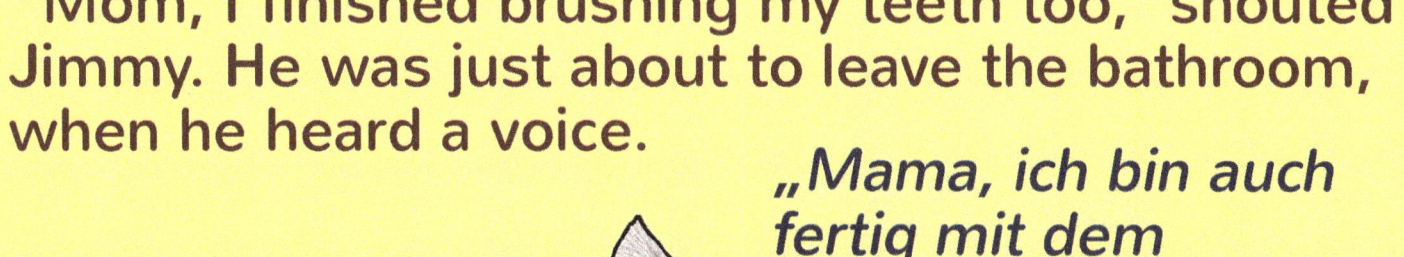

"It's not nice to lie," the voice said. "You didn't brush your teeth."

„Es ist nicht nett zu lügen", sagte die Stimme. „Du hast deine Zähne nicht geputzt."

"Who said that?" asked Jimmy as he looked around in confusion.
"Over here," was the reply.

*„Wer hat das gesagt?", fragte Jimmy, während er verwirrt umherblickte.
„Hier drüben", kam die Antwort.*

Frowning at him was his new orange toothbrush, standing on the counter.

Seine neue orange Zahnbürste stand auf dem Waschbecken und sah ihn schräg an.

"A toothbrush can't talk," he said in a stunned voice.

„Eine Zahnbürste kann nicht sprechen", sagte er mit erstaunter Stimme.

"I sure can. I'm a magical toothbrush," said the toothbrush proudly. "My job is to make sure EVERYONE brushes his teeth."

„Kann ich wohl. Ich bin eine magische Zahnbürste", sagte die Zahnbürste stolz. „Meine Aufgabe ist es, sicherzustellen, dass JEDER seine Zähne putzt."

Jimmy laughed in response. "I didn't brush my teeth and nothing bad happened to me."

Jimmy antwortete mit einem Lachen: „Ich habe meine Zähne nicht geputzt und nichts Schlimmes ist mir passiert."

"Look at yourself," the brush said. "Your teeth are yellow and your breath smells terrible."

„Schau dich selbst an", sagte die Bürste. „Deine Zähne sind gelb und dein Atem riecht schrecklich."

"That's not true, brush. You're just making it up!" Jimmy took the toothbrush and threw it far into the corner of the bathroom.

„Das ist nicht wahr, Bürste, das denkst du dir nur aus!" Jimmy nahm die Zahnbürste und warf sie in die Badezimmerecke.

Then he ran into the kitchen to have his breakfast.

Dann rannte er in die Küche, um zu frühstücken.

"That's no way to treat me," shouted the toothbrush. "I'm a magical toothbrush. I'll prove how important I am!"

„Das ist keine Art, mich zu behandeln", schrie die Zahnbürste. „Ich bin eine magische Zahnbürste. Ich werde dir beweisen, wie wichtig ich bin!"

By this time, Jimmy was already sitting down next to his brothers in the kitchen.

Jimmy setzte sich währenddessen bereits neben seine Brüder in der Küche.

He took a sandwich and brought it to his mouth. But then the sandwich jumped out of Jimmy's hands right onto the plate of his oldest brother.

Er nahm ein Sandwich und wollte hineinbeißen. Doch da sprang das Sandwich aus Jimmys Händen direkt auf den Teller seines ältesten Bruders.

Instead of the sandwich, Jimmy had bitten his fingers — hard!
"Ouch, it hurts!" he yelled.

Anstatt in sein Sandwich, hatte Jimmy in seine Finger gebissen - fest!
„Autsch, das tut weh!", schrie er.

"Who does this sandwich belong to?" the brother asked.

„Wem gehört dieses Sandwich?", fragte der ältere Bruder.

"My sandwich ran away from me," answered Jimmy. "It's mine!"

„Das ist mein Sandwich", antwortete Jimmy. „Es ist vor mir weggelaufen!"

"Quite an imagination you have, sweetie. How can a sandwich run away?" his mother said.

„Du hast aber eine blühende Fantasie, Liebling. Wie kann ein Sandwich weglaufen?", sagte seine Mutter.

"I don't know how, but that's really what happened," said Jimmy.

„Ich weiß es nicht! Aber es ist wirklich weggelaufen", sagte Jimmy.

Then, Mom gave him a big plate full of salad. "Here, perhaps you would like to eat a delicious vegetable salad instead," she said.

Dann gab ihm die Mama einen großen Teller voll Salat. „Hier, vielleicht möchtest du stattdessen lieber einen leckeren Gemüsesalat essen", sagte sie.

"Yummy, I love vegetable salad," said Jimmy, about to start eating. Suddenly, the salad plate leaped up and settled down on the table near his middle brother.

„Lecker, ich liebe Gemüsesalat", sagte Jimmy und wollte anfangen zu essen. Plötzlich sprang der Salatteller auf und landete auf dem Tisch bei seinem mittleren Bruder.

"Look," said the middle brother, "how did your plate get over here?"

„Schau", sagte der mittlere Bruder, „wie ist dein Teller hier hingekommen?"

"You were right, honey! Your food is running away from you!" said their astonished mom. "That's strange."

„Du hattest Recht, Schatz! Dein Essen rennt vor dir weg!", sagte ihre erstaunte Mama. „Das ist merkwürdig."

"Mom, I'm getting hungry already. What can I eat?" said Jimmy.

„Mama, ich bekomme wirklich Hunger. Was kann ich essen?", fragte Jimmy.

Mom thought for a moment. "How about your favorite carrot cake? I'll give you a big slice."

Mama dachte einen Moment nach. „Wie wäre es mit deinem Lieblingskarottenkuchen? Ich werde dir ein großes Stück geben."

"Oh yes, carrot cake! I love it so much," Jimmy shouted happily, "Thanks, Mom."

„Oh ja, Karottenkuchen! Den liebe ich so sehr", rief Jimmy glücklich, „Danke, Mama."

However, before Jimmy could take the cake, it began to float in the air. It flew into the living room and settled on the couch.

Bevor Jimmy allerdings den Kuchen nehmen konnte, begann dieser, in der Luft zu schweben. Er flog ins Wohnzimmer und landete auf der Couch.

Jimmy hopped out of his chair and started chasing the piece of cake. He jumped on the sofa, but the cake zoomed back to the table.

Jimmy hüpfte von seinem Stuhl und begann, das Kuchenstück zu jagen. Er sprang auf das Sofa, aber der Kuchen sauste zurück zum Tisch.

Jimmy ran back to the table and then the cake flew out of the house. Jimmy rushed after it. The cake looped around the house while Jimmy trailed behind it.

Jimmy rannte zum Tisch zurück, aber der Kuchen flog aus dem Haus. Der Kuchen flog um das Haus herum, während Jimmy ihm folgte.

Another round and another and another, and still Jimmy followed.

Eine Runde, und noch eine Runde, und Jimmy verfolgte ihn noch immer.

Until he had run out of breath. Tired, Jimmy sat down at the entrance of the house and started crying.

Bis er außer Atem war. Müde setzte sich Jimmy in den Hauseingang und fing an zu weinen.

At the same moment, two of his friends were passing by.

Im gleichen Moment kamen zwei seiner Freunde vorbei.

"Hey, Jimmy," they greeted. "Why are you sitting here looking so sad? Come play with us."

„Hey, Jimmy", begrüßten sie ihn. „Warum sitzt du hier und siehst so traurig aus? Komm, spiel mit uns."

"Yes, I'd like that!" Jimmy ran towards them. "You won't believe what happened to me today!"

„Ja, das würde ich gern!" Jimmy rannte ihnen entgegen. „Ihr werdet nicht glauben, was mir heute passiert ist!"

But, as he opened his mouth, the friends shouted, "Yikes, what a stink! We'll go play somewhere else while you go brush your teeth!" With that, they ran away.

Aber als er seinen Mund öffnete, riefen seine Freunde: „Igitt, was für ein Gestank! Wir werden woanders spielen gehen, während du deine Zähne putzen gehst!" Damit rannten sie weg.

Bursting into tears yet again, Jimmy entered the house. He went to the bathroom and saw the magical toothbrush flying in the air, smiling kindly at him.

Jimmy brach erneut in Tränen aus und ging ins Haus. Er lief ins Badezimmer und sah die magische Zahnbürste in der Luft fliegen. Sie lächelte ihn freundlich an.

"Hello, Jimmy. I've been waiting for you. Do you want to brush your teeth now?" Jimmy nodded.

„Hallo, Jimmy. Ich habe auf dich gewartet. Möchtest du jetzt deine Zähne putzen?" Jimmy nickte.

Jimmy started brushing his teeth, from one side to the other, top and bottom, front and back.

Jimmy fing an, seine Zähne zu putzen. Von einer Seite zur anderen, oben und unten, vorne und hinten.

He brushed them until they became white and shiny.

Er putzte sie, bis sie weiß und glänzend waren.

Gazing proudly at his reflection in the mirror, Jimmy said, "Thank you, brush. It was even nice and pleasant to brush my teeth. I now have sweet-smelling breath too."

Jimmy blickte stolz sein Spiegelbild an und sagte: „Danke, Bürste. Es war sogar schön und angenehm, meine Zähne zu putzen. Jetzt habe ich auch einen frischen Atem."

"You look great," said the brush. "By the way, my name is Leah. I'm always here to help."

„Du siehst toll aus", sagte die Bürste. „Übrigens, mein Name ist Leah. Ich bin immer hier, um zu helfen."

That's how Jimmy and Leah became good friends.

So wurden Jimmy und Leah gute Freunde.

Ever since that day, they've seen each other twice a day to protect Jimmy's teeth and help them grow strong and healthy.

Seit diesem Tag sehen sie sich täglich zweimal, um Jimmys Zähne zu schützen und ihnen dabei zu helfen, kräftig und gesund zu wachsen.

www.ingramcontent.com/pod-product-compliance
Lightning Source LLC
Chambersburg PA
CBHW061130070526
44584CB00033B/4284